THE CLASSICAL GUITAR COLLECTION
GEORGE GERSHWIN

WISE PUBLICATIONS
PART OF THE MUSIC SALES GROUP

LONDON / NEW YORK / PARIS / SYDNEY / COPENHAGEN / BERLIN / MADRID / HONG KONG / TOKYO

PUBLISHED BY
WISE PUBLICATIONS
14-15 BERNERS STREET,
LONDON W1T 3LJ, UK.

EXCLUSIVE DISTRIBUTORS:
MUSIC SALES LIMITED
DISTRIBUTION CENTRE, NEWMARKET ROAD,
BURY ST EDMUNDS, SUFFOLK,
IP33 3YB, UK.

MUSIC SALES PTY LIMITED
20 RESOLUTION DRIVE, CARINGBAH,
NSW 2229, AUSTRALIA.

ORDER NO. AM1003101
ISBN 978-1-78038-013-1
THIS BOOK © COPYRIGHT 2011
WISE PUBLICATIONS,
A DIVISION OF MUSIC SALES LIMITED.

UNAUTHORISED REPRODUCTION OF
ANY PART OF THIS PUBLICATION BY ANY
MEANS INCLUDING PHOTOCOPYING
IS AN INFRINGEMENT OF COPYRIGHT.

MUSIC ARRANGED BY JERRY WILLARD.
MUSIC PROCESSED BY PAUL EWERS MUSIC DESIGN.
CD PERFORMED AND RECORDED BY JERRY WILLARD.

CD MIXED AND MASTERED BY JONAS PERSSON.

PRINTED IN THE EU.

WWW.MUSICSALES.COM

DO, DO, DO 7

DO IT AGAIN 10

I GOT RHYTHM 12

IDLE DREAMS 15

I'LL BUILD A STAIRWAY TO PARADISE 18

LIZA (ALL THE CLOUDS'LL ROLL AWAY) 19

LOOKING FOR A BOY 22

MY MAN'S GONE NOW 26

OH, LADY, BE GOOD 29

'S WONDERFUL 32

SCANDAL WALK 34

SO AM I 38

SOMEONE TO WATCH OVER ME 41

SUMMERTIME 44

SWANEE 46

SWEET AND LOW DOWN 48

THAT CERTAIN FEELING 52

CD TRACK LISTING 56

JERRY WILLARD

Born in Cleveland, Ohio, Jerry Willard's first teacher was his father, Jeff Willard, an accomplished guitarist in his own right. The guitar pedagogue Sophocles Papas recognized Jerry's talent and invited him to study in Washington, D.C. Jerry Willard studied with guitarists Richard Lurie and Alirio Diaz, who developed his musical and technical approach to the guitar. He also worked with violinist Misha Mishakoff and cellist Warren Downs who expanded his knowledge of musical interpretation.

Mr. Willard has performed at Alice Tully Hall and Carnegie Hall in New York City. He has performed extensively throughout Europe and The United States. Raymond Ericson of the New York Times wrote, "The recital was exemplary. Mr. Willard took lute in hand for some pieces by Adrian LeRoy and John Dowland and turned that normally pale-sounding predecessor of the guitar into a brilliant and vivid instrument…It was again the clarity of Mr. Willard's playing that gave special pleasure."

Willard is an accomplished player of all types of fretted instruments including the archlute, Renaissance lute, Baroque guitar, 19th-century guitar, and modern guitar. Well-known as an ensemble player, Mr. Willard has performed with the Cleveland Orchestra, The New York Opera Company, The New York Consort of Viols and The Queen's Chamber Band.

Willard has published many publications for guitar including *The Complete Lute Music of J.S. Bach* and *The Complete Works of Gaspar Sanz*, both available through Wise Publications. Mr. Willard records for Lyrichord Discs. He has recorded music for archlute, Baroque Guitar and Renaissance lute. He has just finished a recording of opera potpourris by Giuliani and Mertz on a Lacote guitar made in Paris in 1820. Mr. Willard resides in New York City and is on the faculty of the State University of New York at Stony Brook.

PREFACE

My first teacher was my father, an amateur guitarist in the 1920s and 30s. He taught me by rote to play songs of that era, many of which are included in this book. He would play the melody and I would play the chords and then we'd switch. When I first heard a fingerstyle guitarist play both the melody and the accompaniment at the same time I was enchanted – amazed – and it changed my life forever. These early guitar experiences eventually led me to create the arrangements in this book.

Gershwin for Classical Guitar is the culmination of many years of arranging and playing these Gershwin songs in concerts and recitals, adding and pruning them as the situation demanded. My focus on these Gershwin arrangements is not to make a 'jazz' version, or to deal in chord substitutions, but to arrange them in a period style, as they would have been heard in the 1920s and the 30s.
Gershwin came out of ragtime and Tin Pan Alley traditions and many of his arrangements and his piano playing reflect that; stride and 'walking' bass styles lend themselves neatly to fingerstyle guitar playing.

Arranging is always a subjective process, especially in transferring virtuosic piano music to the smaller limitations of the guitar. For this reason I have kept the music as lean and simple as I could while still maintaining the gesture and style of the songs. Ideally when a passage is meant to convey simplicity then the passage as played on the guitar should be easy to play. This is not always possible or practical, but I have tried to come as close as possible to that ideal. When passages were encountered that were beyond the limitations of the guitar in their original form I have adjusted them to something suited to the guitar to convey the musical gesture that I felt Gershwin was after.

In order to maintain a good bass and full sound on the guitar the key centres that I have used are limited to three: D, G and A. These keys help enormously with their open strings. The negative aspect of this is a redundancy of the same keys in performance or recording. If this becomes a problem I would recommend a capo one or two frets up to give the key flexibility required.

Most of the fingering is pretty straightforward and in keeping with current conventions. The exception to this is a barring device I use called a **cross bar** (abbreviated **CB**) where the index finger is in a barring position and playing two notes at different frets.

In this example from 'Looking For A Boy' (page 24) the cross bar happens on the last two beats of the measure. My suggestion is to bar normally at the 5th fret; while maintaining the A on top curve your index finger forward and grab the D♯. You can also try the opposite way and fret the chord as if there were no bar at all and then let the index finger fall down on the neck to fret the 1st string A. After a little practice you will find this easy to do.

Standard rhythmic notation is limited in its capacity to display music which is to be swung; this creates discrepancies between what is written and the way it is actually played. Usually when two eighth notes are written this way:

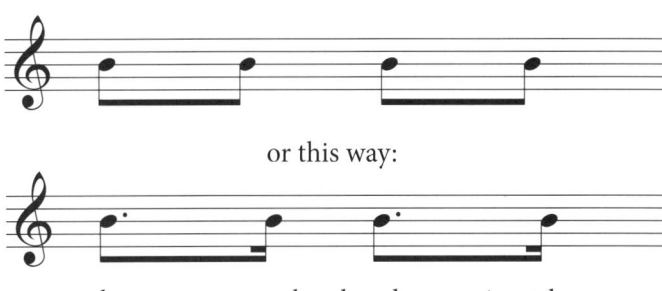

or this way:

they are meant to be played approximately:

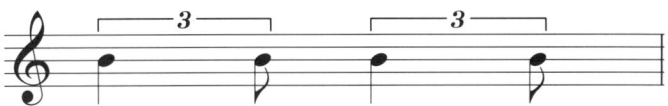

to give it a swing. There are no hard or fast rules about swing or rhythmic flexibility. Usually I swing the eighth notes but there are times, especially for emphasis or in slower ballads, when I will play it as written. This is dependant on one's own musical style and aesthetic.

My source materials for this book were the Gershwin Songbook, Gershwin piano vocal scores, Gershwin's own piano roll recordings and the big band arrangements by Paul Whiteman.

I would like to thank Tom Farncombe and the Music Sales editorial staff for their fine work and help in the final production of this book. Also Jonas Persson for the final mastering and production of the enclosed CD.

Jerry Willard
New York City
April 2011

YOUR GUARANTEE OF QUALITY:

AS PUBLISHERS, WE STRIVE TO PRODUCE EVERY BOOK
TO THE HIGHEST COMMERCIAL STANDARDS.

THIS BOOK HAS BEEN CAREFULLY DESIGNED TO MINIMISE AWKWARD
PAGE TURNS AND TO MAKE PLAYING FROM IT A REAL PLEASURE.
PARTICULAR CARE HAS BEEN GIVEN TO SPECIFYING ACID-FREE, NEUTRAL-SIZED PAPER
MADE FROM PULPS WHICH HAVE NOT BEEN ELEMENTAL CHLORINE BLEACHED.
THIS PULP IS FROM FARMED SUSTAINABLE FORESTS AND WAS PRODUCED
WITH SPECIAL REGARD FOR THE ENVIRONMENT.

THROUGHOUT, THE PRINTING AND BINDING HAVE BEEN PLANNED TO ENSURE
A STURDY, ATTRACTIVE PUBLICATION WHICH SHOULD GIVE YEARS OF ENJOYMENT.

IF YOUR COPY FAILS TO MEET OUR HIGH STANDARDS,
PLEASE INFORM US AND WE WILL GLADLY REPLACE IT.

DO, DO, DO

MUSIC BY GEORGE GERSHWIN
ARRANGED BY JERRY WILLARD

© COPYRIGHT 2011 DORSEY BROTHERS MUSIC LIMITED.
ALL RIGHTS RESERVED. INTERNATIONAL COPYRIGHT SECURED.

DO IT AGAIN

MUSIC BY GEORGE GERSHWIN
ARRANGED BY JERRY WILLARD

I GOT RHYTHM

MUSIC BY GEORGE GERSHWIN
ARRANGED BY JERRY WILLARD

IDLE DREAMS

MUSIC BY GEORGE GERSHWIN
ARRANGED BY JERRY WILLARD

I'LL BUILD A STAIRWAY TO PARADISE

MUSIC BY GEORGE GERSHWIN
ARRANGED BY JERRY WILLARD

© COPYRIGHT 2011 DORSEY BROTHERS MUSIC LIMITED.
ALL RIGHTS RESERVED. INTERNATIONAL COPYRIGHT SECURED.

LIZA (ALL THE CLOUDS'LL ROLL AWAY)

MUSIC BY GEORGE GERSHWIN
ARRANGED BY JERRY WILLARD

LOOKING FOR A BOY

MUSIC BY GEORGE GERSHWIN
ARRANGED BY JERRY WILLARD

MY MAN'S GONE NOW

MUSIC BY GEORGE GERSHWIN
ARRANGED BY JERRY WILLARD

OH, LADY, BE GOOD

MUSIC BY GEORGE GERSHWIN
ARRANGED BY JERRY WILLARD

'S WONDERFUL

MUSIC BY GEORGE GERSHWIN
ARRANGED BY JERRY WILLARD

© COPYRIGHT 2011 DORSEY BROTHERS MUSIC LIMITED.
ALL RIGHTS RESERVED. INTERNATIONAL COPYRIGHT SECURED.

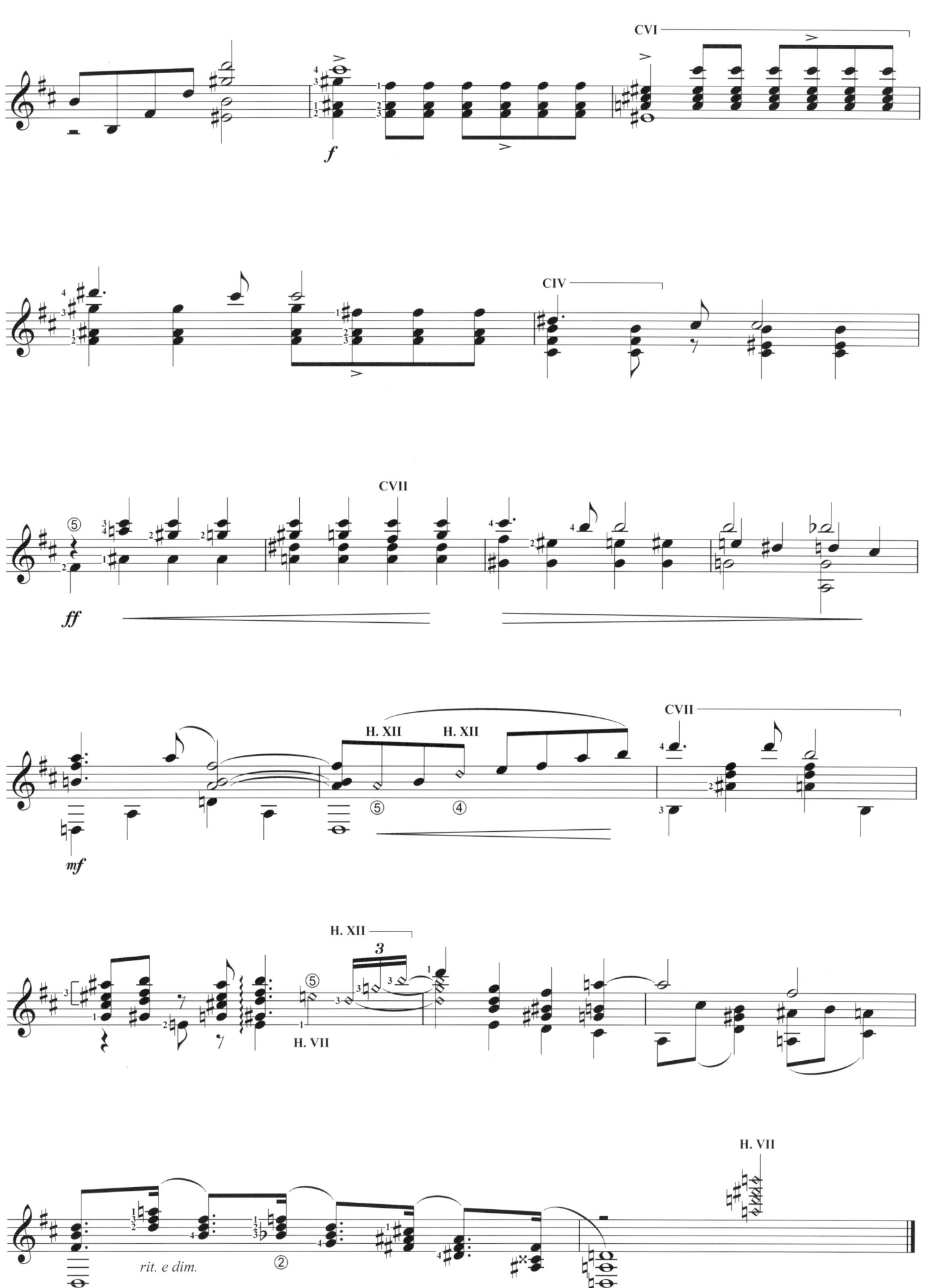

SCANDAL WALK

MUSIC BY GEORGE GERSHWIN
ARRANGED BY JERRY WILLARD

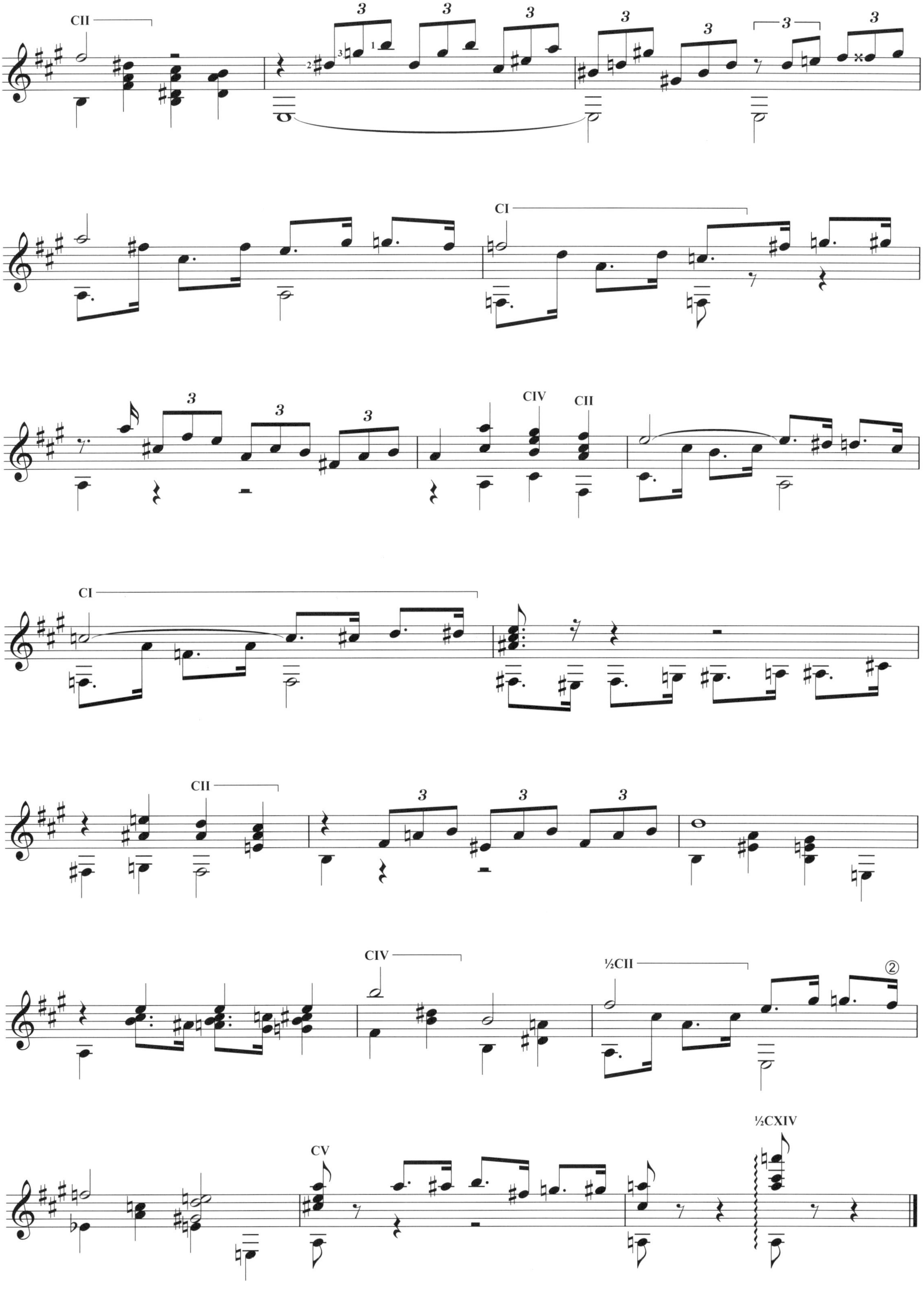
CII
CI
CIV
CII
CI
CII
CIV
½CII
CV
½CXIV

SO AM I

MUSIC BY GEORGE GERSHWIN
ARRANGED BY JERRY WILLARD

A tempo
½CVII
½CV
½CII
mp
CII
rit.
CII
CIV
CII
CII
CVII
rit.
A tempo
CII
CII
CII
allarg.
½CVII
½CV
CII
mp
CBI
CII
½CVII
rit.
A tempo
½CVII
CII
½CVII
CII
(mp)
CII
CI

½CVII
CII
CII
CVII
CII
CIV
CII
CII
CVII
CII
CII
½CVII
CII
½CVII
rit.
A tempo
mp
CVI
rit.
½CVII
H. VII

SOMEONE TO WATCH OVER ME

MUSIC BY GEORGE GERSHWIN
ARRANGED BY JERRY WILLARD

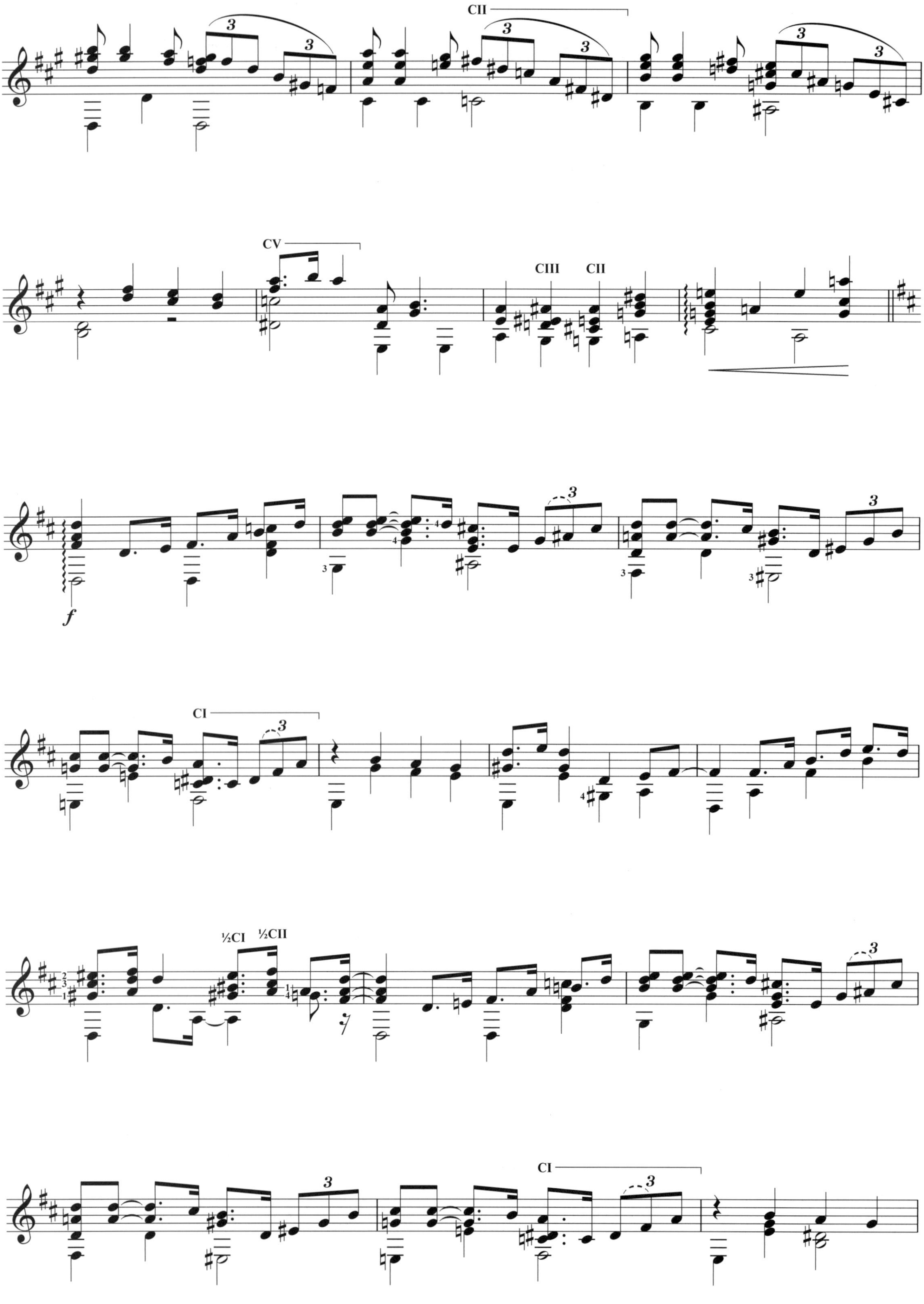
CII
CV
CIII
CII
f
CI
½CI
½CII
CI

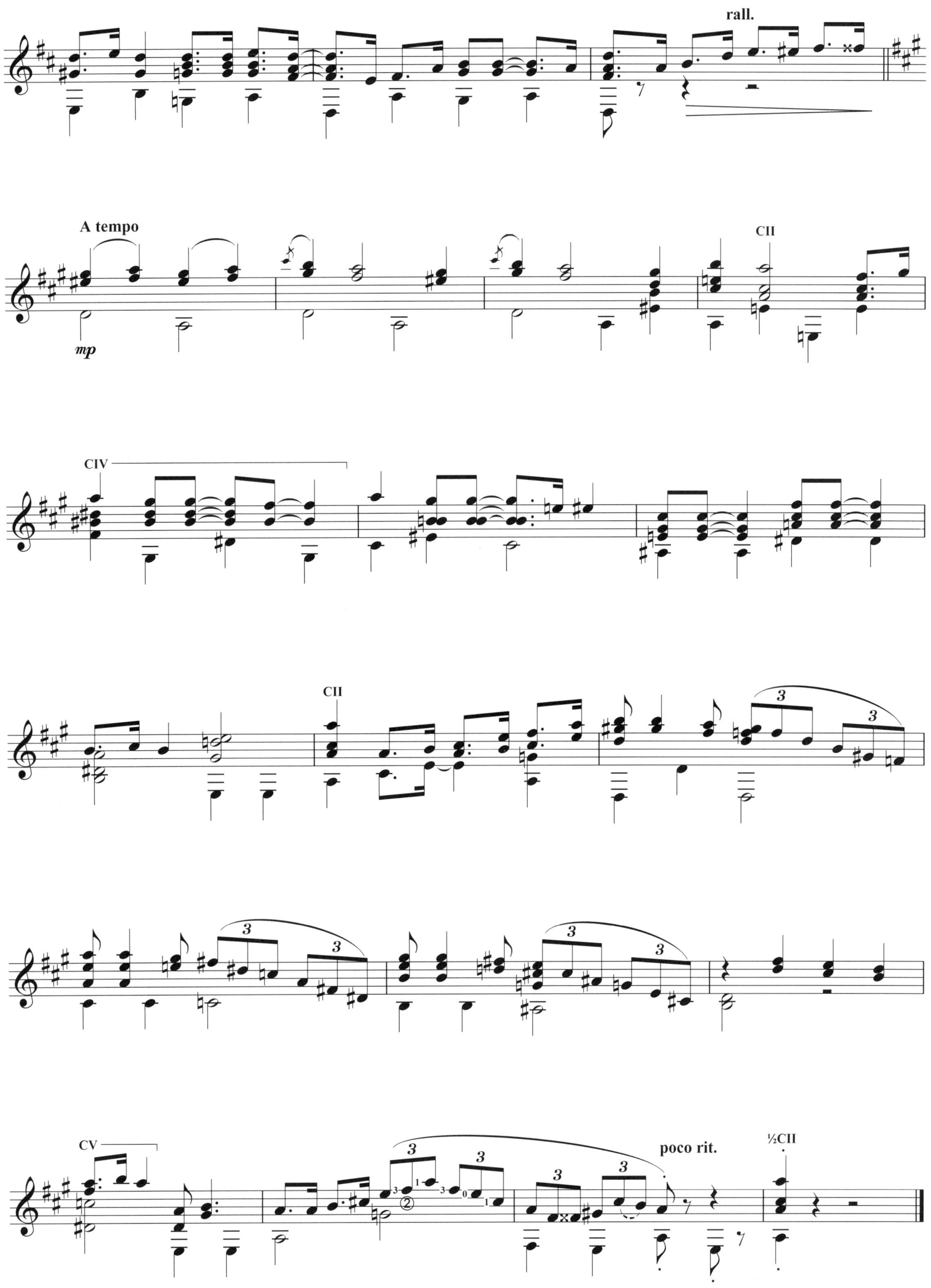
rall.
A tempo
mp
CII
CIV
CII
CV
poco rit.
½CII

SUMMERTIME

MUSIC BY GEORGE GERSHWIN
ARRANGED BY JERRY WILLARD

*fret F# on first string; play harmonic at 21st fret

© COPYRIGHT 2011 DORSEY BROTHERS MUSIC LIMITED.
ALL RIGHTS RESERVED. INTERNATIONAL COPYRIGHT SECURED.

CII
H. 8va
H. 8va
H. 8va
CII
CII
CII
CII
½CIII
CII
CII
CII
CIII
H. XII
pp

SWANEE

MUSIC BY GEORGE GERSHWIN
ARRANGED BY JERRY WILLARD

cresc.
sf
ff
mf
molto cresc.
a i m p
CIX
f
CVII
CV
CIV
CII
1.
CVI
CV
2.
mf
p
pp

SWEET AND LOW DOWN

MUSIC BY GEORGE GERSHWIN
ARRANGED BY JERRY WILLARD

© COPYRIGHT 2011 DORSEY BROTHERS MUSIC LIMITED.
ALL RIGHTS RESERVED. INTERNATIONAL COPYRIGHT SECURED.

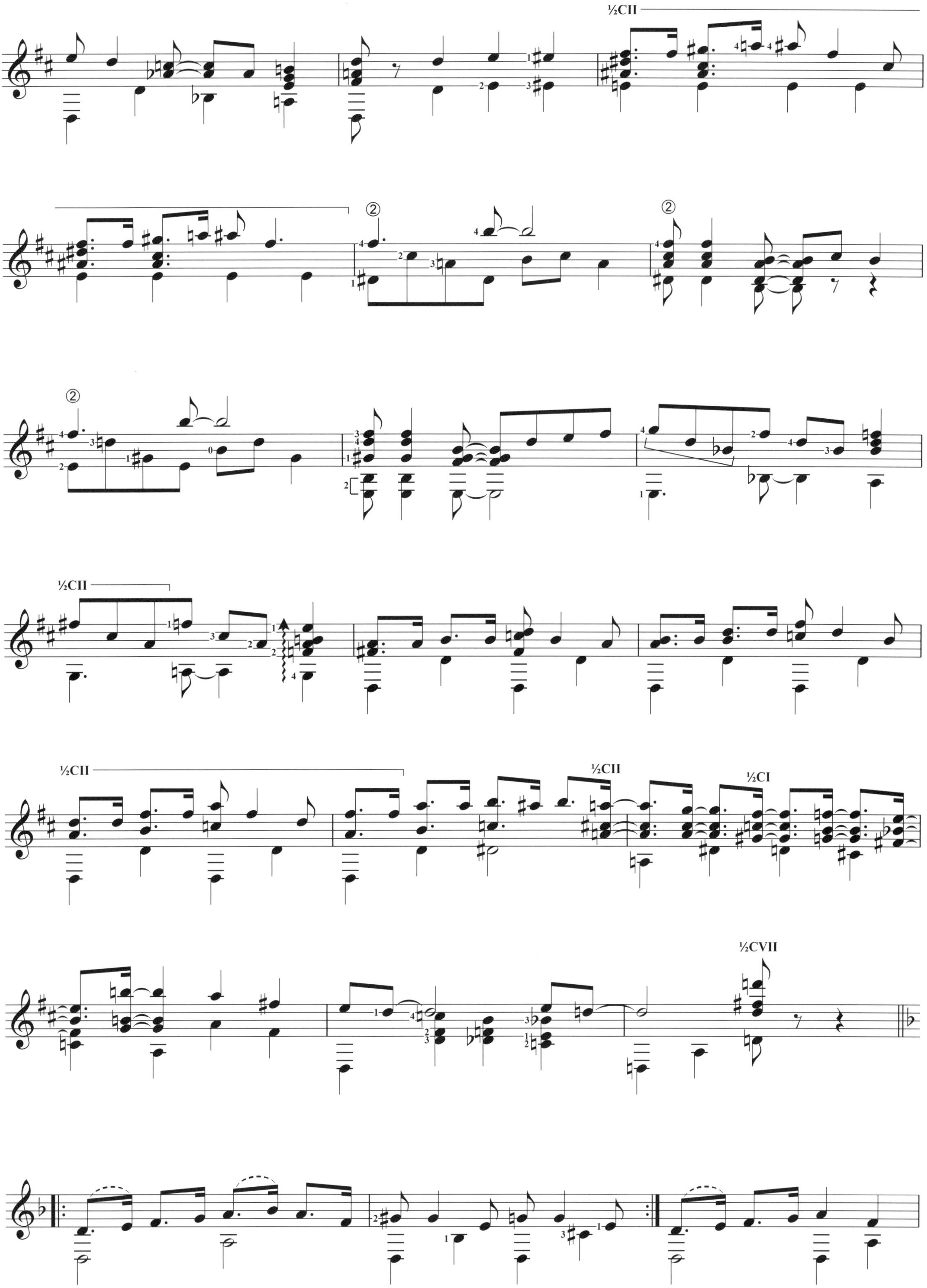
½CII
②
②
②
½CII
½CII
½CII
½CI
½CVII

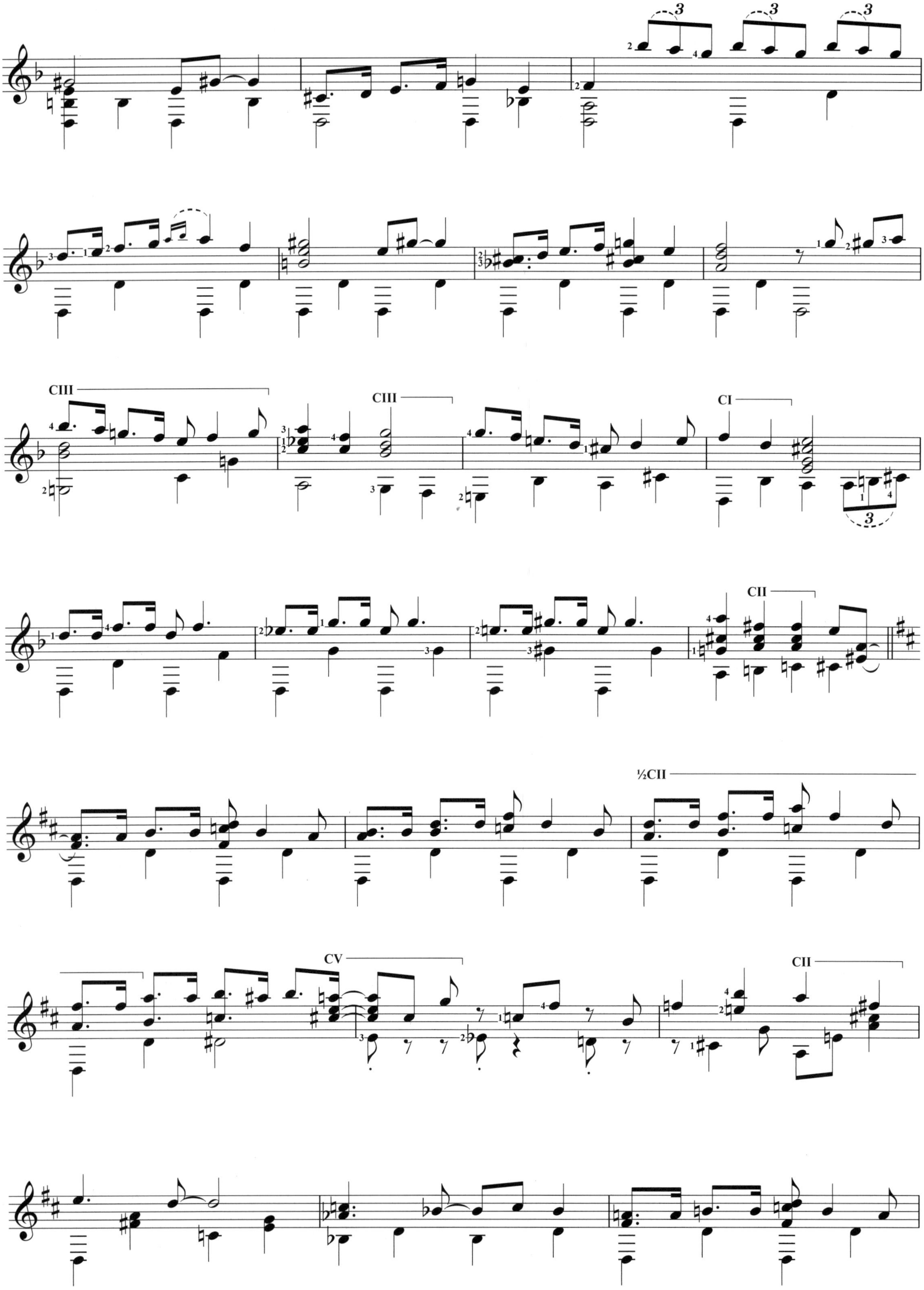
CIII
CIII
CI
CII
½CII
CV
CII

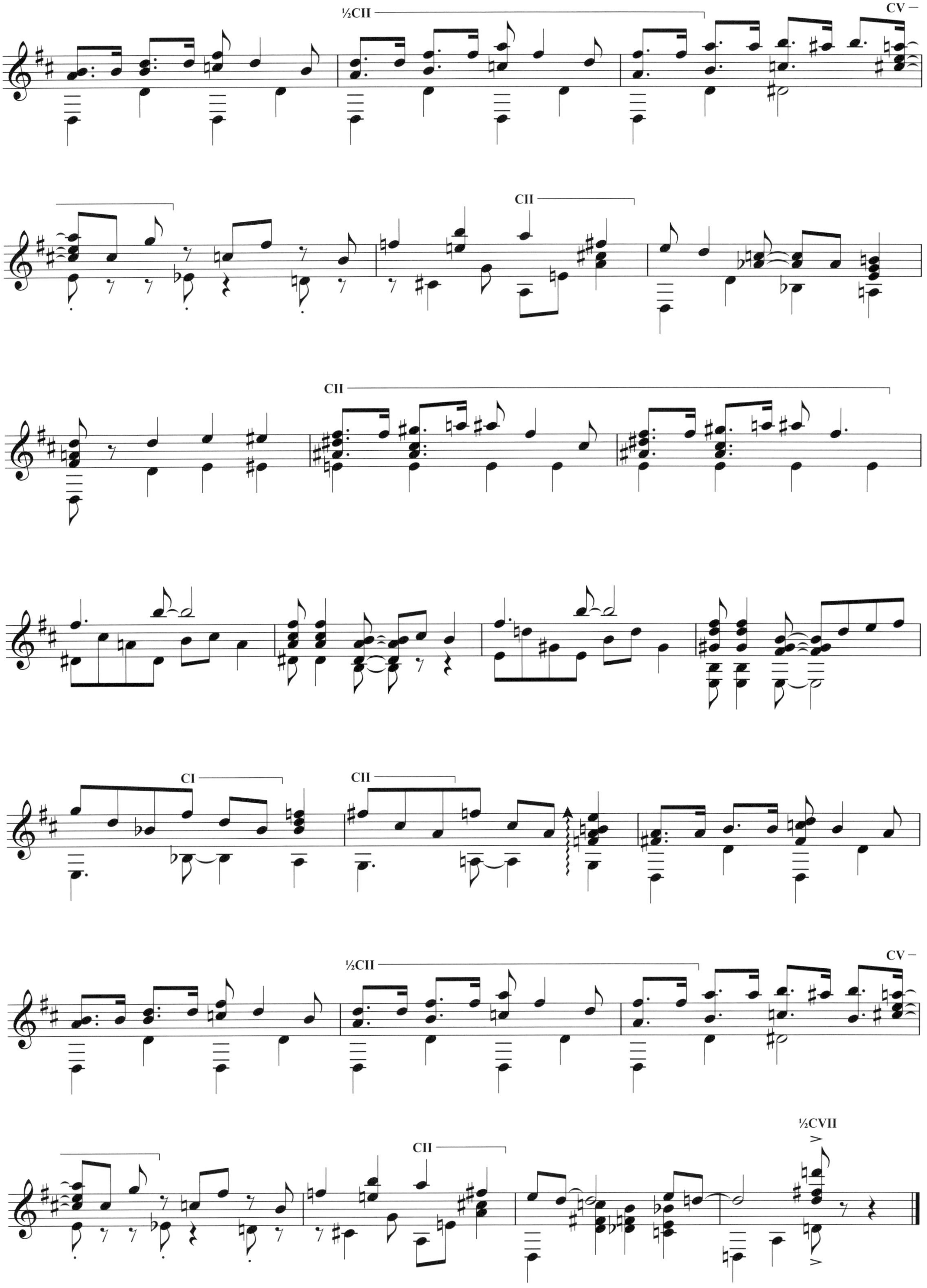
½CII
CV
CII
CII
CI
CII
½CII
CV
CII
½CVII

THAT CERTAIN FEELING

MUSIC BY GEORGE GERSHWIN
ARRANGED BY JERRY WILLARD

½CI
½CII
f
f
mp
½CII
f
a piacere
CII
rall.
Meno mosso
CII
½CII
mp
CII

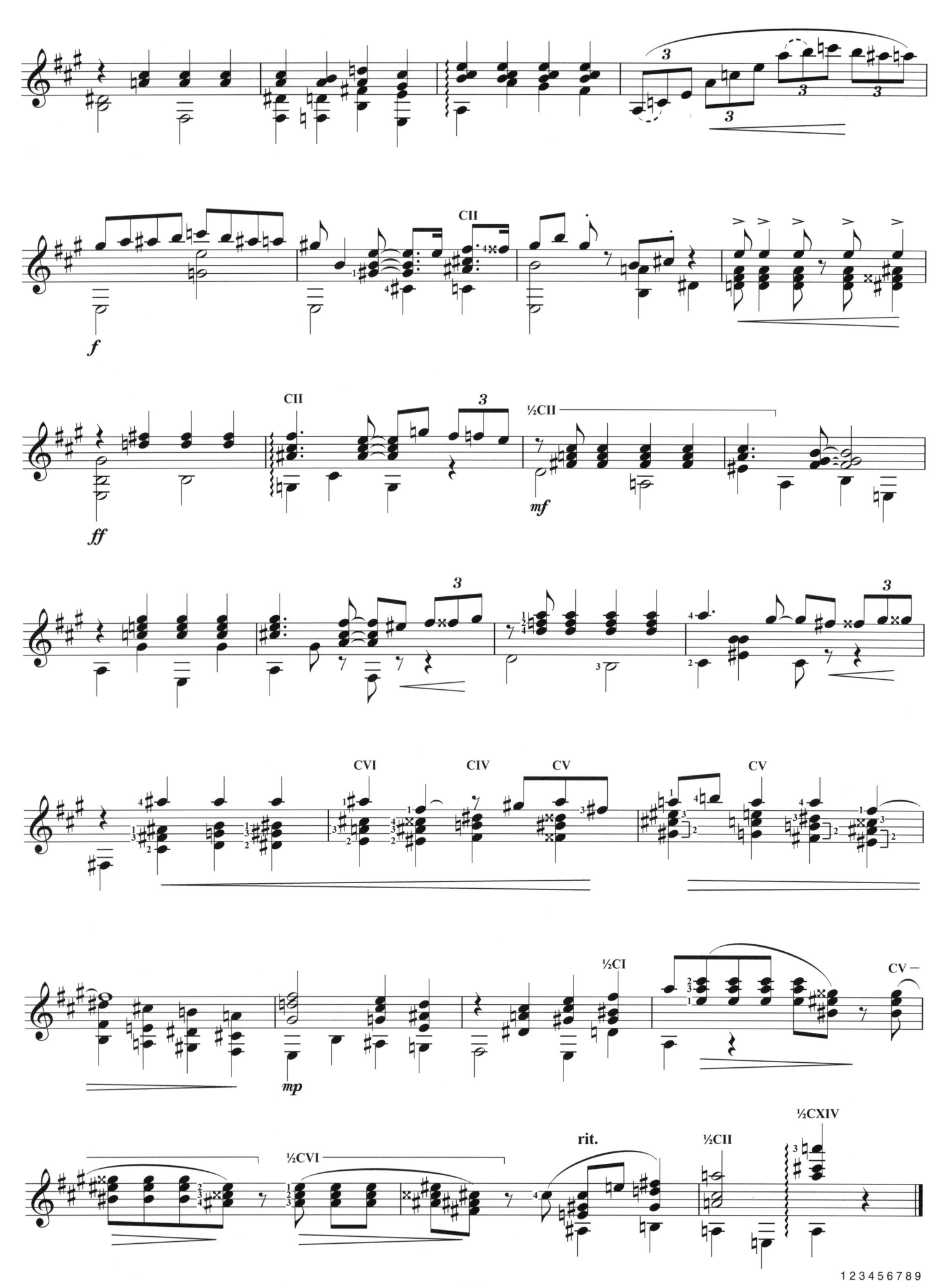

1 2 3 4 5 6 7 8 9

CD TRACK LISTING

1. DO, DO, DO
(GERSHWIN)
DORSEY BROTHERS MUSIC LIMITED

2. DO IT AGAIN
(GERSHWIN)
DORSEY BROTHERS MUSIC LIMITED

3. I GOT RHYTHM
(GERSHWIN)
DORSEY BROTHERS MUSIC LIMITED

4. IDLE DREAMS
(GERSHWIN)
DORSEY BROTHERS MUSIC LIMITED

5. I'LL BUILD A STAIRWAY TO PARADISE
(GERSHWIN)
DORSEY BROTHERS MUSIC LIMITED

6. LIZA (ALL THE CLOUDS'LL ROLL AWAY)
(GERSHWIN)
DORSEY BROTHERS MUSIC LIMITED

7. LOOKING FOR A BOY
(GERSHWIN)
DORSEY BROTHERS MUSIC LIMITED

8. MY MAN'S GONE NOW
(GERSHWIN)
DORSEY BROTHERS MUSIC LIMITED

9. OH, LADY BE GOOD
(GERSHWIN)
DORSEY BROTHERS MUSIC LIMITED

10. 'S WONDERFUL
(GERSHWIN)
DORSEY BROTHERS MUSIC LIMITED

11. SCANDAL WALK
(GERSHWIN)
DORSEY BROTHERS MUSIC LIMITED

12. SO AM I
(GERSHWIN)
DORSEY BROTHERS MUSIC LIMITED

13. SOMEONE TO WATCH OVER ME
(GERSHWIN)
DORSEY BROTHERS MUSIC LIMITED

14. SUMMERTIME
(GERSHWIN)
DORSEY BROTHERS MUSIC LIMITED

15. SWANEE
(GERSHWIN)
DORSEY BROTHERS MUSIC LIMITED

16. SWEET AND LOW DOWN
(GERSHWIN)
DORSEY BROTHERS MUSIC LIMITED

17. THAT CERTAIN FEELING
(GERSHWIN)
DORSEY BROTHERS MUSIC LIMITED